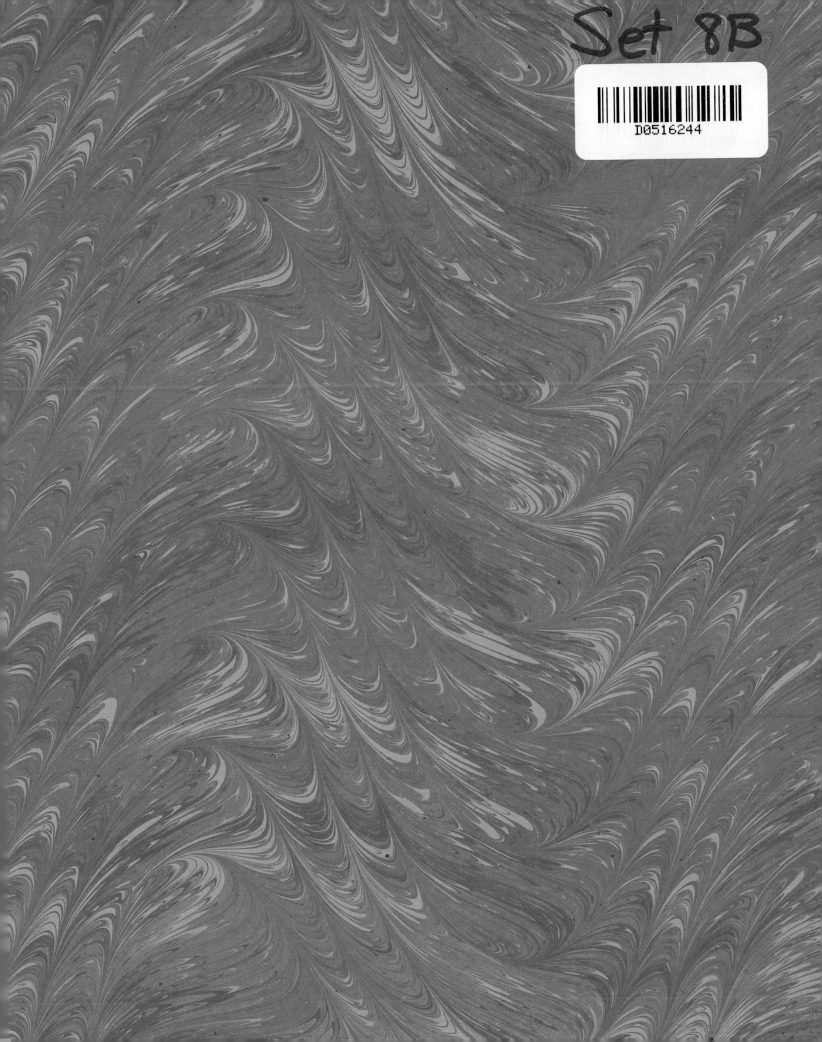

Set 8B

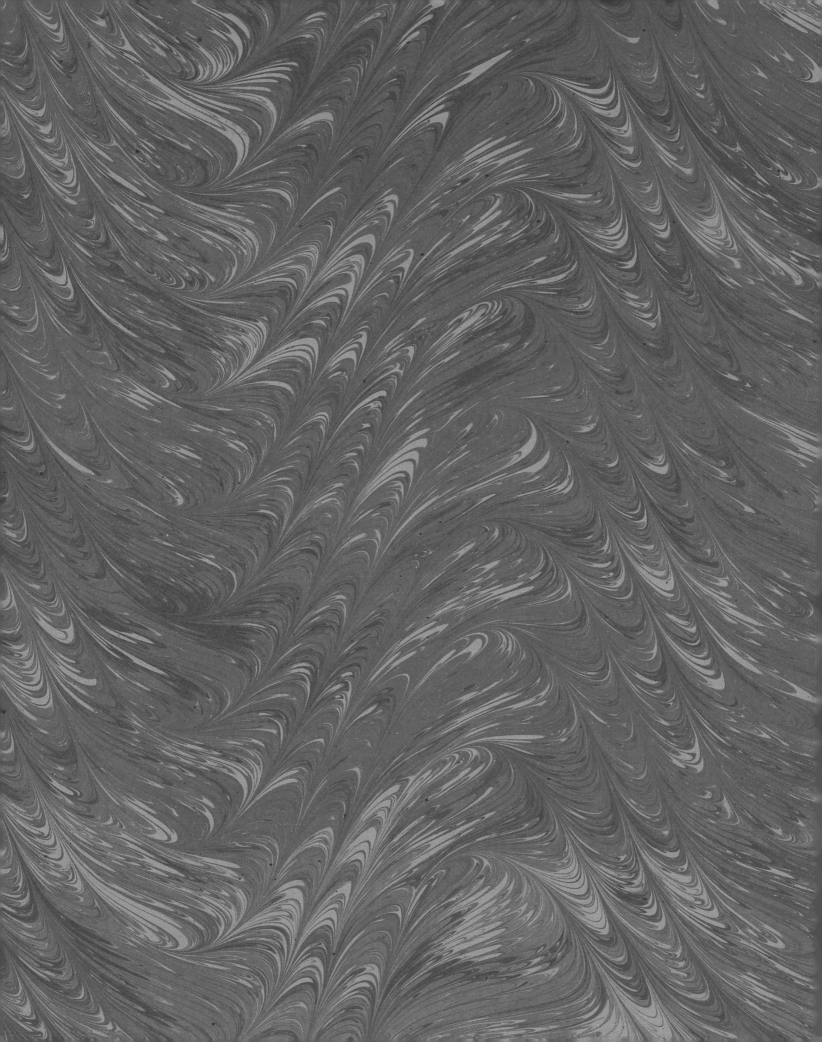

HARCOURT
· TROPHIES ·

A HARCOURT READING/LANGUAGE ARTS PROGRAM

CATCH A DREAM

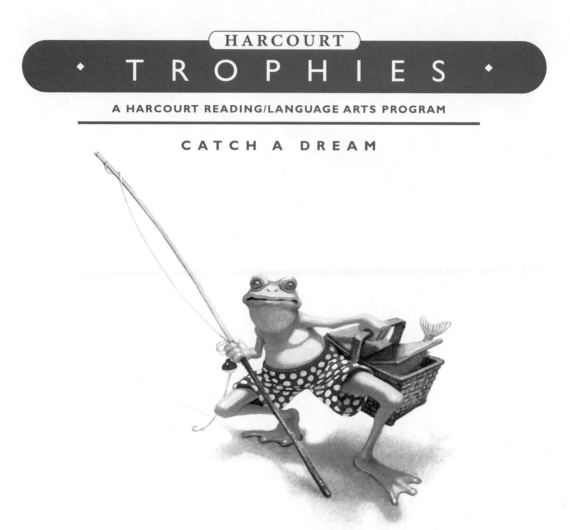

SENIOR AUTHORS
Isabel L. Beck ◆ Roger C. Farr ◆ Dorothy S. Strickland

AUTHORS
Alma Flor Ada ◆ Marcia Brechtel ◆ Margaret McKeown
Nancy Roser ◆ Hallie Kay Yopp

SENIOR CONSULTANT
Asa G. Hilliard III

CONSULTANTS
F. Isabel Campoy ◆ David A. Monti

Harcourt

Orlando   Boston   Dallas   Chicago   San Diego

Visit *The Learning Site!*

www.harcourtschool.com

HARCOURT

· T R O P H I E S ·

A HARCOURT READING/LANGUAGE ARTS PROGRAM

C A T C H   A   D R E A M

Dear Reader,

This book has stories about real animals that grow and change. It has stories about imaginary animals, too — some who are silly and some who are super! It also has stories about children just like you who love their pets and learn to always try their best. So turn the page and **Catch a Dream!**

Sincerely,

The Authors

The Authors

It's My Turn Now

CONTENTS

Reading **Across** Texts

Theme Big Books

Decodable Books 7-12

THEME
3

It's
My Turn
Now

▲ Dan's Pet

Word Power

Words to Remember

day

every

her

said

was

with

8

Where **was** Dan?
"I **was with** my pet," **said** Dan. "I call **her** Jen. I go to see her **every day**."

9

Genre

Realistic Fiction

Realistic fiction stories are about things that could really happen.

Look for:

- Events that can happen in real life.
- People as characters.

by Alma Flor Ada
illustrated by Brian Karas

10

Dan's Pet

Dan held a small baby chick.

It was soft in his hands.

"Can I have her as a pet?"

"Yes, Dan," said Mama.

"I'll call her Jen," said Dan.

Dan helped with Jen.

Dan fed Jen and all the hens.

Dan fed Jen every day.

Jen got very big!

One day, Dan didn't see Jen.
"Jen! Jen!" Dan called.

"Jen is in here," said Mama.
"Look at her eggs."

"Oh, my!" said Dan.
"Now I will have lots of pets!"

Think and Respond

1 What is Dan's pet?

2 What does Dan's pet do?

3 Is Dan surprised? How can you tell?

4 Why will Dan have lots of pets now?

5 Would you like to have pets like Dan's? Why or why not?

Meet the Author
Alma Flor Ada

Alma Flor Ada has always loved to write about nature. As a child, she spent hours near a river watching plants, insects, birds, and frogs. Now she lives in a small house near a lake, where she still enjoys watching the world of nature.

Brian Karas

Brian Karas lives near many farms. He thought about the chickens that he sees on the farms as he drew the pictures for "Dan's Pet."

Brian Karas has illustrated more than 60 books. His two sons give him many ideas for his pictures. They love to draw and paint, just like their dad!

Brian Karas

SEE HOW THEY GROW
CHICK

How a Chick Grows

The egg

One hour old

Three days old

Eight days old

Two weeks old

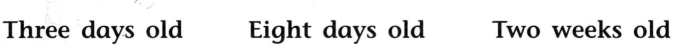

Four weeks old   **Eight weeks old**

Making Connections

Dan's New Pets

Make up a story about the new baby chicks. The mother hen's name is Jen. Name all the chicks, too!

Writing
CONNECTION

28

How Many Legs?

**Math
CONNECTION**

How many legs does a hen have? How many legs does a pig have? Make a list of farm animals. Then write those animal names in a chart like this.

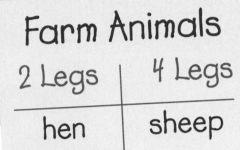

Farm Animals

2 Legs	4 Legs
hen	sheep

Farm Animal Song

**Music
CONNECTION**

Sing this song together. Then make up new verses with different animal names.

**The farmer has a hen.
The farmer has a hen.
Hi, ho, the derry-o,
The farmer has a hen.**

Setting

The **setting** of a story is where that story takes place.

This picture shows the setting of "Dan's Pet." Is the setting a farm, a ranch, or a city? How can you tell?

Test Prep
Setting

Where Are You?

It has lots of cans.

It has lots of bags.

You can buy food here.

What is the setting?

- ○ a pond
- ○ a hill
- ○ a store

Tip

Read the sentences very carefully before you choose your answer.

Word Power

Words to Remember

could

friends

new

put

she

use

Beth's **friends** got her
a **new** hat.
She put it on.
She said, "It's too
big for me.
I think Meg **could
use** this hat."

Genre

Fantasy

A fantasy is a
make-believe story.

Look for:

- Animal characters
that talk and act
like people.

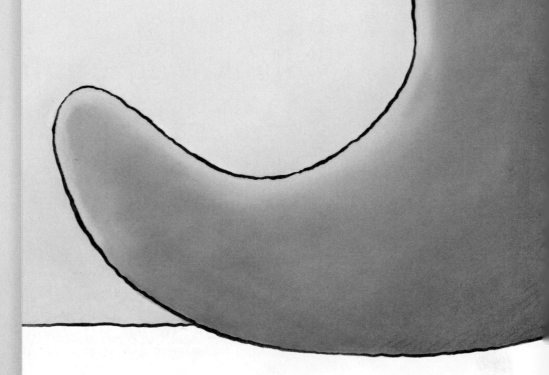

Boots for Beth

by Lisa Campbell Ernst

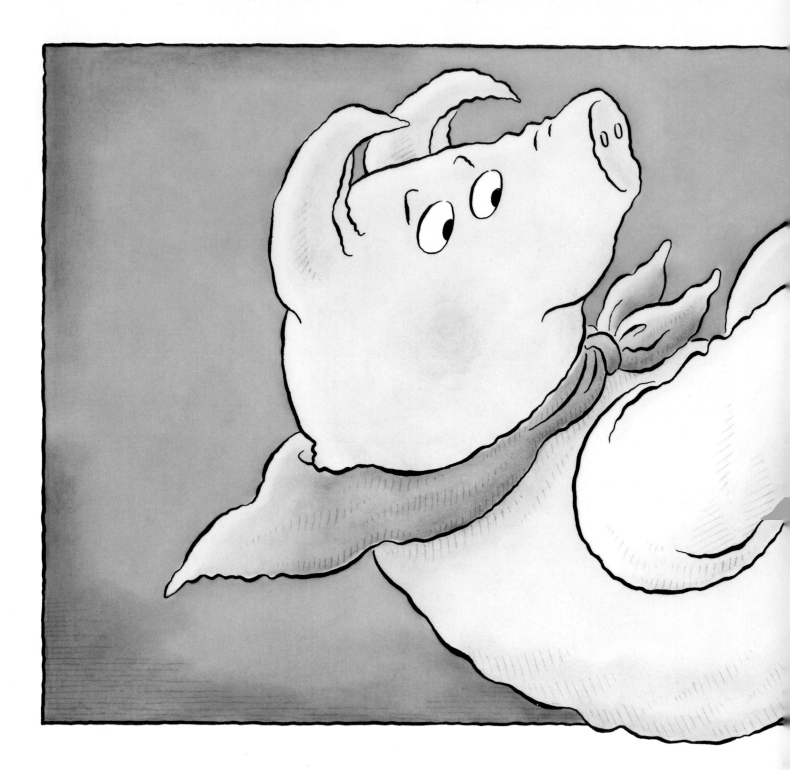

Beth was sad.

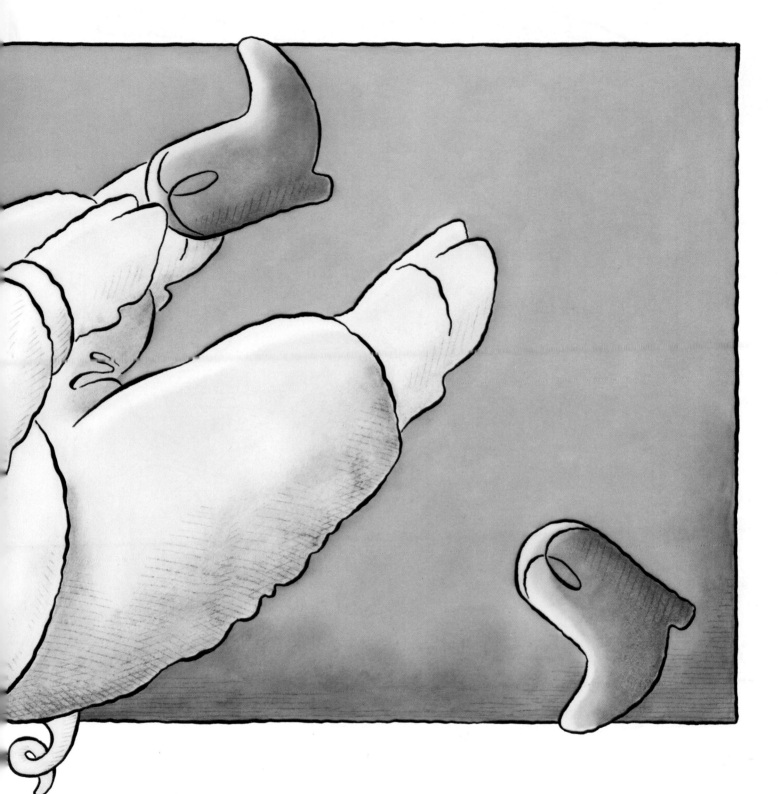

"My red boots don't fit," she cried.
"I can not get them on."

"Could you use my boots?"
asked Meg.

"They are too big," said Beth.

"Will my boots fit?" asked Ned.

"Too small," said Beth.

"Could you use my pink boots?"
asked Liz.

"Too soft," said Beth.

"Will my boots help?" asked Ted.

"Too wet," said Beth.

"Can you put on my black boot?"
asked Jeff.

"It is too thin," said Beth.

Beth still felt sad.
Her friends all felt bad.

They got a big surprise for Beth.

"New red boots!"
said Beth. "Thanks!"

"Hop on," said Meg.
"Let's play!"

Think and Respond

1. What problem does Beth have?

2. How is Beth's problem solved?

3. What happens first in the story? What happens last?

4. How can you tell that Beth's friends are nice?

5. Have you ever had a problem like Beth's? What did you do?

Meet the Author/Illustrator

Lisa Campbell Ernst

Lisa Campbell Ernst got the idea for "Boots for Beth" while shopping for shoes with her own two children. "How sad we feel when a favorite pair of shoes no longer fits!" she says. "Then the search for just the right new pair begins. Some shoes are too big, too small, or too stiff. At last you find just the right ones!"

Lisa Campbell Ernst

Making Connections

Thank-You Note

It's nice to write a note when you get a gift. Pretend you are Beth. Thank your friends for the new boots. Share your work.

Writing CONNECTION

From: Beth

To: My friends

Thank You!

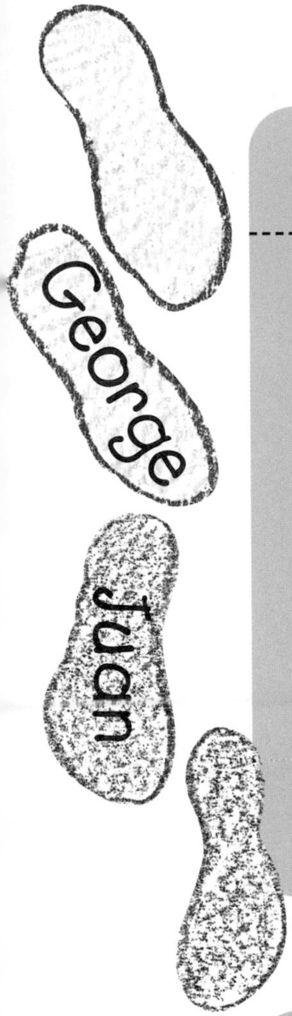
George
Juan

Foot Fun

Math CONNECTION

Work with a few classmates. Stand on paper. Have one person trace around your shoes. When everyone has a set of "footprints," cut them out. Put them in order from smallest to biggest.

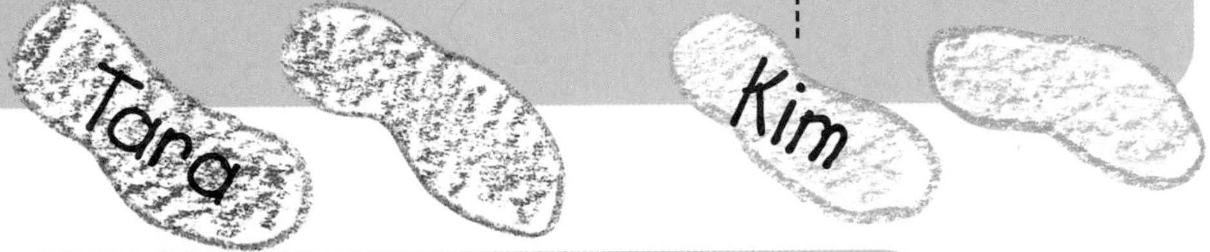
Tara
Kim

Boots Around the World

Social Studies CONNECTION

Look at pictures of people who live in very cold places. What do they wear on their feet? Draw a picture of the warm boots they wear.

Words with <u>th</u> (Phonics Skill)

The letters <u>th</u> together stand for the /th/ sound at the beginning of <u>thanks</u> and at the end of <u>Beth</u>.

Here are some words with <u>th</u> that you read in "Boots for Beth."

thin   them   they

Say the words <u>tin</u> and <u>thin</u>. Write both words.

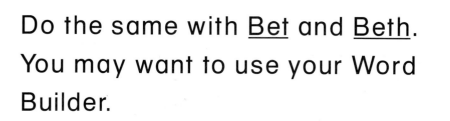

Do the same with <u>Bet</u> and <u>Beth</u>. You may want to use your Word Builder.

56

Test Prep

Words with <u>th</u>

1. **Which word has the sound for <u>th</u> in the beginning?**

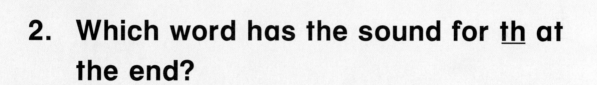

○   ○   ○

2. **Which word has the sound for <u>th</u> at the end?**

○   ○   ○

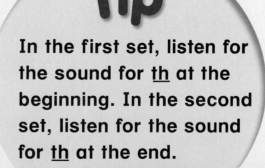

Tip

In the first set, listen for the sound for <u>th</u> at the beginning. In the second set, listen for the sound for <u>th</u> at the end.

▲ Space Pup

Word Power

Words to Remember

gives

he

night

out

people

says

when

your

Gus isn't like **your** dog. **When night** comes, Gus is **out**. He **gives** help to **people**. **He says**, "Here I come!"

space

Fantasy

A fantasy is a make-believe story.

Look for:

- Characters that have super powers.

- Amazing events.

PUP

by Robert Cooker
illustrated by Julia Gorton

Gus the Pup rests all day.

Gus can not rest at night.
Gus is Space Pup!

Space Pup helps people.
"Here I come," yells Space Pup.

Space Pup sees a bus. He says,
"The bus is stuck in the mud!"

"Here I come!" yells Space Pup.

He sees people stuck in the bus!

"The bus is stuck!" they yell.
"Help us, Space Pup!"

"Hand me your rope," says
Space Pup.

"What will you do with it?" asks
the man.

"I'll get the bus out of the mud," says Space Pup.

Space Pup runs and runs.
He gives the rope a big tug.

"You did it, Space Pup!"
they yell.

Space Pup is the best!

Space Pup helps people at night,

but when the sun comes up,

Gus the Pup rests all day.

Think and Respond

1 What does Gus do all day?

2 What does Gus do at night?

3 What does Space Pup do on the night of this story?

4 If you had been on the bus, what would you have done?

5 Why do you think Gus is called Space Pup?

Meet the Illustrator

Julia Gorton

Gus the Space Pup works hard to help people and so does Julia Gorton. She works to make her community a better place. She is trying to get a skateboard park built in her town. She wants children to have a safe place to skateboard.

Julia Gorton drew Gus to look strong and cheerful. She used an airbrush to paint the bright colors. What do you think of her pictures?

julia gorton

▲ Space Pup

Making Connections

Real-Life Help

Gus pulled a bus out of the mud all by himself! If a bus got stuck where you live, how would it be pulled out? Talk about your ideas.

Social Studies CONNECTION

More Help from Space Pup

Writing CONNECTION

Think about another way Space Pup could help people. Write about it. Draw a picture.

HELP!

Real Dogs

Science/ Technology CONNECTION

Learn something new about dogs. Draw and write about what you learn.

Short Vowel <u>u</u>

The letter <u>u</u> can stand for the /u/ sound. Say <u>pup</u>. The /u/ sound is the short sound of <u>u</u>.

Name these pictures. What sound do you hear in the middle?

Name these pictures. Which picture does **<u>not</u>** have the short sound of <u>u</u> in the middle?

82

Test Prep
Short Vowel u

1. **Which picture name has the short sound of u?**

○   ○   ○

2. **Which picture name has the short sound of u?**

○   ○   ○

Tip

Say /u/. Say the picture name slowly. Does the picture name have the /u/ sound?

Word Power

**Words to
Remember**

eat

from

gone

grows

or

two

A frog **grows** fast.
You'll see where frogs come **from**.
You'll see what frogs **eat**, too.
Look at this frog's **two** long legs.
Look fast, **or** the frog is **gone**!

Where

Genre

Nonfiction

A nonfiction story tells about things that are real.

Look for:

- Animal photographs.
- Lots of information.

Do Frogs

Come From?

by Alex Vern

Frogs come <mark>from</mark> small eggs.

The black things on this
plant are frog eggs.

Pop! Pop!
A tadpole pops out
of an egg.

Pop, pop, pop!
Lots and lots of tadpoles pop
out. A tadpole has to swim
fast or a fish could eat it!

The tadpole has a long
tail and a big body.

It looks for plants
in the pond. It eats
the plants and
grows a lot.

It grows two strong back legs.
They help the tadpole kick fast
and swim.

It grows two small front legs, too. The tadpole is now a frog that has a tail.

Now the tadpole is a big strong frog. Its long tail is gone, so it can hop.

Hop, hop! Plop, plop!

The frog is fast. It eats lots of bugs. The bugs are not as fast as the frog!

From Egg to Frog

1. Egg

2. Tadpole

3. Frog

Think and Respond

1. What did you learn about frogs?

2. What is a frog called when it pops out of its egg?

3. What are three changes that happen to a tadpole?

4. What surprised you about how frogs grow?

5. What else would you like to learn about frogs?

Meet a Photographer
Gary Meszaros

Gary Meszaros is a nature photographer. He loves taking pictures of birds and fish. Some days he spends hours wading in cold streams and lakes. Other days, he brings tadpoles, fish, and insects into his studio. The photographs he took for "Where Do Frogs Come From?" were done in his studio.

Polliwogs

by Kristine O'Connell George
illustrated by Jui Ishida

Come see
What I found!
Chubby commas,
Mouths round,
Plump babies,
Stubby as toes.
Polliwogs!
Tadpoles!

Come see
What I found!
Frogs-in-waiting—
Huddled in puddles,
Snuggled in mud.

Making Connections

Frog or Toad?

Learn how frogs are different from toads. Share what you find out. Help make a class chart about frogs and toads.

Science/ Technology CONNECTION

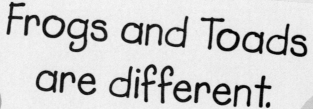

Frogs and Toads are different.

Frogs	Toads
live in water smooth skin	live on land rough skin

104

Frog Pond Picture

Make a big picture of a frog pond. Show frogs jumping and catching bugs. Add plants and other animals.

Art CONNECTION

A Tadpole Tale

Lots of things happen in a tadpole's life! Make up a story about a tadpole. It can be real or make-believe.

Writing CONNECTION

Details

As you read, remember the important **details**. Doing this will help you understand what you read.

Read this. Think about the important details.

A tadpole has a tail. It swims in the pond. It eats plants and grows a lot.

What does the tadpole do that makes it grow?

- It swims in the pond.
- It uses its tail.
- It eats plants.

106

Test Prep
Details

The Frog

The frog sat on a rock in the sun. The frog got hot. It jumped into the pond.

1. What did the frog do when it got hot?

○ It slept in the sun.

○ It jumped into the pond.

○ It jumped onto a rock.

Tip

Think about which detail tells what the frog did when it felt hot.

▲ Try Your Best

Word Power

Words to Remember

be

good

Mr.

need

our

right

saw

time

try

Jan and Ann are **good** friends.
Jan **saw** Ann looking sad.
Mr. York said, "It's **time** for **our** day camp."

"I don't want to **be** at camp," said Ann.

"You just **need** to **try**!" said Jan.

Jan is **right**. Ann needs to **try**.

Genre

Realistic Fiction

Realistic fiction stories are about things that could really happen.

Look for:

- **Characters that seem like people you could meet.**

- **Activities that could have happened to you or someone you know.**

Try Your Best

by Robert McKissack

illustrated by Joe Cepeda

"It's Sports Day," said Mr. York.

"Oh, good!" said Jan.

"Oh, no!" said Ann. "I don't
think I'm very good at sports."

"Just try your best, Ann," said
Mr. York.

"It's time for you to kick, Ann,"
said Mr. York.

"Oh, no!" said Ann.

"What a kick!" said Mort.
"You helped us score."

"See, Ann?" said Mr. York.
"You can do it."

"Next you will climb the rope,"
said Mr. York.

"Oh, no!" said Ann.

"Good job, Ann!" said Mr. York.

"Now it's time to run a race."

"We need one more to play,"
said Jan.

"Can you be on our team,
Mr. York?" asked Ann.

"Oh, no!" said Mr. York. "I don't
think I can run very fast."

"Just try your best!" said Ann.

"You are right, Ann," said
Mr. York. "I'll just try my best!"

Mr. York started to run. Just
then he saw a big frog. He ran
very, very fast!

"Run, Mr. York!" called Mort.

"Go, Mr. York!" yelled Ann.

"I did my best!" said Mr. York.

"Yes, Mr. York," said Ann.
"You AND the frog did your best!"

Think and Respond

1 Why doesn't Ann want to play on Sports Day?

2 What do both Ann and Mr. York learn?

3 What makes Mr. York run so fast?

4 Which of the Sports Day games would you like best?

5 Do you like the way the story ends? Why or why not?

Meet the Author
Robert McKissack

Robert McKissack thought about his summer camp days when he wrote "Try Your Best." Some of the children were afraid to try new things. They missed out on all the fun! He thinks all children should try their best. "Reach for the stars," he tells them. "You may go there someday!"

Robert McKissack

Little fish are **food** for big fish. **Some** little fish **hide** from big fish. **Many** little fish just swim **away** fast.

Some fish look **funny** to us. **How** do **some** fish help **their** friends? You'll see!

135

Genre

Nonfiction

Nonfiction describes books of information and fact.

Look for:

- **Photographs that help explain.**

- **Information that is easy to find.**

Fun with Fish

by Jane Ward

photographs by Norbert Wu

Put on some flippers.
Put on a mask.

Jump in and swim
down,
down,
down.

What will you see?

Fish! Fish! Fish!

What helps fish swim?

Tails and fins help fish swim.
Swish, swish, swish!
Fish swish their tails.

What do fish eat?

Some fish eat plants.

Many big fish eat small fish.

How do small fish get away?

Some fish hide in sand.
Some hide in plants.

This frog fish hides too.
Can you see all the fish?

Some fish look funny. This fish is called a clown fish.

Some fish look mad.
This fish has big teeth.

This fish is small. It can puff up to make fish go away.

Puff, puff, puff! Now it is big!

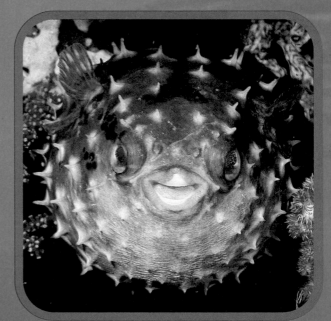

Some fish are friends. The long fish eats bits of food off its big friend's skin.

This fish is helping the diver.
CLICK!
Thank you, fish!

Think and Respond

1. What is the diver doing in this story?

2. The story tells about two things fish eat. What are they?

3. How do some fish hide so well?

4. Which fish did you think was the most interesting? Why?

5. How do you think the photographer feels about fish?

About the Photographer

Norbert Wu

Norbert Wu takes pictures in the cold waters of Antarctica and in the warm waters around coral reefs. Where do you think he was when he took the pictures for "Fun with Fish"?

The Sharks

Sharks can park
Wherever they wish.
They do not fear
The other fish.
Sharks can swim
Wherever they please.
On this each other
Fish agrees.

by Douglas Florian
illustrated by Barry Gott

Making Connections

A Fish Story

Choose one fish from "Fun with Fish." Write about your fish. Draw a picture, too.

Writing
CONNECTION

The big red fish had three baby fish. They went for a swim.

One day Puffer saw a shark! He puffed up and the shark swam away!

What a Neat Fish!

Look at some fish in books. Pick a fish you really like. Find out something about your fish. Share what you learn.

Science
CONNECTION

A Fish Dinner

Many fish are good to eat. What would you serve with fish? Draw a healthful fish dinner!

Health
CONNECTION

159

Details

When you read "Fun with Fish," you need to remember important **details**.

Do you remember what a fish uses to swim? Which of these answers is right?

Visit *The Learning Site!*
www.harcourtschool.com

See *Skills* and *Activities*

- **flippers and a mask**
- **teeth**
- **tails and fins**

Test Prep
Details

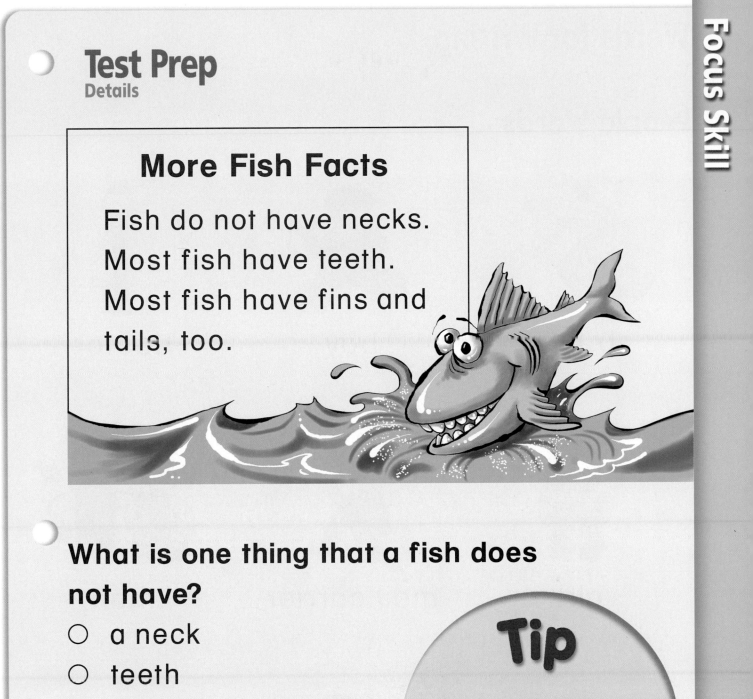

More Fish Facts

Fish do not have necks.
Most fish have teeth.
Most fish have fins and
tails, too.

What is one thing that a fish does not have?

- ○ a neck
- ○ teeth
- ○ a tail

Tip

Read all the sentences.
Then read the question
very carefully before
you answer.

Words for Writing

People Words

baby

boy

doctor

girl

mail carrier

man

police officer

teacher

woman

Color Words

black

blue

brown

green

orange

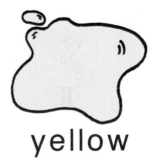

purple

red

yellow

Words for Writing

Place Words

airport

beach

city

farm

library

neighborhood

school

store

Animal Words

bird

cat

cow

dog

fish

horse

bear

frog

rabbit

snake

Glossary

What is a Glossary?

A glossary can help you read a word. You can look up the word and read it in a sentence. Each word has a picture to help you.

fast   The truck can go **fast**.

eat   I like to **eat** hot dogs.

fast   The truck can go **fast**.

fins   **Fins** help fish swim.

friends   My **friends** sang a song to me.

funny   The puppy did a **funny** trick.

hand   Mom's **hand** is bigger than my hand.

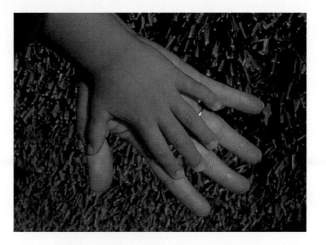

hen   The **hen** has six eggs.

hide   I can **hide** from you.

jump   **Jump** over the mud.

kick   Sam can **kick** the ball.

mask   My **mask** looks like a rabbit.

night   The sun is not out at **night**.

people   Ten **people** are on the bus.

small   That hat is too **small**.

strong   The **strong** man can lift the big box.

172

swim   Nell can **swim** fast!

thin   The red line is **thin**. The purple line is thick.

Acknowledgments

For permission to reprint copyrighted material, grateful acknowledgment is made to the following sources:

Clarion Books, a Houghton Mifflin Company imprint: "Polliwogs" from *The Great Frog Race and Other Poems* by Kristine O'Connell George. Text copyright © 1997 by Kristine O'Connell George.

Harcourt, Inc.: "The Sharks" from *In the Swim* by Douglas Florian. Text copyright © 1997 by Douglas Florian.

Lodestar Books, an affiliate of Dutton Children's Books, an imprint of Penguin Putnam Books for Young Readers, a division of Penguin Putnam Inc.: "See how I grew" (Retitled: "How a Chick Grows") from *See How They Grow: Chick* by Angela Royston, photographs by Jane Burton, line drawings by Rowan Clifford. Copyright © 1991 by Dorling Kindersley Limited, London.

Photo Credits

Key: (t)=top; (b)=bottom; (c)=center; (l)=left; (r)=right

Page 24, Dale Higgins; 25, Black Star; 26-27(all), Jane Burton / DK Publishing; 53, Nick Vedros; 78, Black Star; 84(t), John Mielcarek / Dembinsky Photo Associates; 84(b), Joe McDonald / Animals Animals; 85, Stephen Dalton / Photo Researchers, Inc.; 86, Stephen Dalton / Animals Animals; 86-87, John Mielcarek / Dembinsky Photo Associates; 88-89, Joyce Photographics / Photo Researchers, Inc.; 89, Hans Pfletschinger / Peter Arnold, Inc.; 90, K. Atkinson / OSF / Animals Animals; 91, William H. Mullins / Photo Researchers, Inc.; 92, Gary Meszaros / Dembinsky Photo Associates; 93, Sharon Cummings / Dembinsky Photo Associates; 94, C. Allan Morgan / Peter Arnold, Inc.; 95, Gary Meszaros / Dembinsky Photo Associates; 96-97, Stephen Dalton / Photo Researchers, Inc.; 98(l), E. R. Degginger / Animals Animals; 98(r), Stephen Dalton / Animals Animals; 99(t), Hans Pfletschinger / Peter Arnold, Inc.; 99(c), Hans Pfletschinger / Peter Arnold, Inc.; 99(r), Joe McDonald / DRK Photo; 100, Jim Battles / Dembinsky Photo Associates; 101(t), Joe McDonald / Animals Animals; 101(b), Steve Meszaros; 128, Black Star; 129, Peter Stone / Black Star; 134, 137(all), Norbert Wu; 138(inset), Robert Essel / Corbis Stock Market; 138-139, 140-148(all), Norbert Wu; 149, Marilyn Kazmers / Peter Arnold, Inc.; 148-149, 150(t), 150(b), 150-151, Norbert Wu; 151, Marilyn Kazmers / Dembinsky; 152-160(all), Norbert Wu; 166, 167(both), Mug Shots / Corbis Stock Market; 168, Kelvin Aitken / PhotoEdit; 169, Amy Dunleavy; 170(t), Robert Brenner / PhotoEdit; 170(b), T&D McCarthy / Corbis Stock Market; 171, Bill Varie / Corbis; 172, Ken Kinzie / Harcourt; 173, Superstock.

Illustration Credits

S. Saelig Gallagher, Cover Art; Larry Reinhart, 4-7; Brian Karas, 8-25; Marina Thompson, 28-29; Liz Callen, 31; Lisa Campbell Ernst, 32-53; Taia Morley, 54, 83; Steve Björkman, 55-56, 80-81; Steve Haskamp, 57; Julia Gorton, 58-79; Jui Ishida, 102-103; Stacy Peterson, 104-105; Alissa Imre Geis, 105; Jo Lynn Alcorn, 107; Joe Cepeda 108-129; C. D. Hullinger, 130-131; Christine Mau, 131; Nancy Davis, 132-133; Barry Gott, 156-157; Eldon Doty, 158-159, 161.

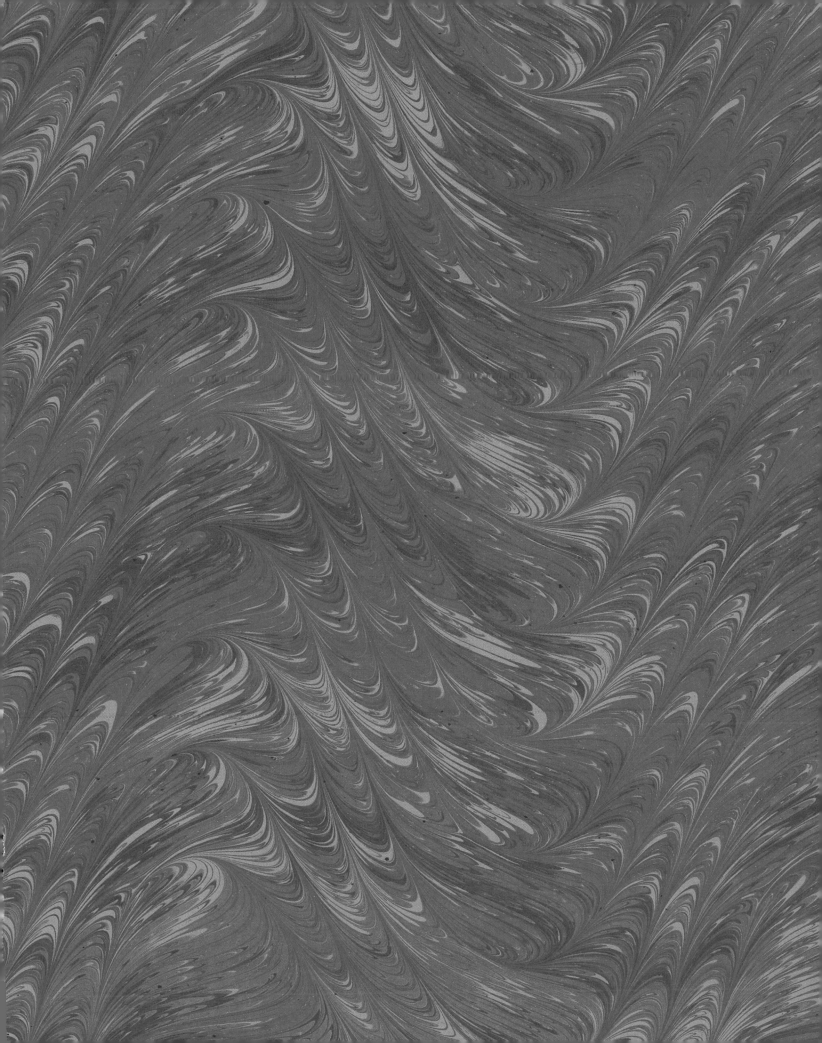

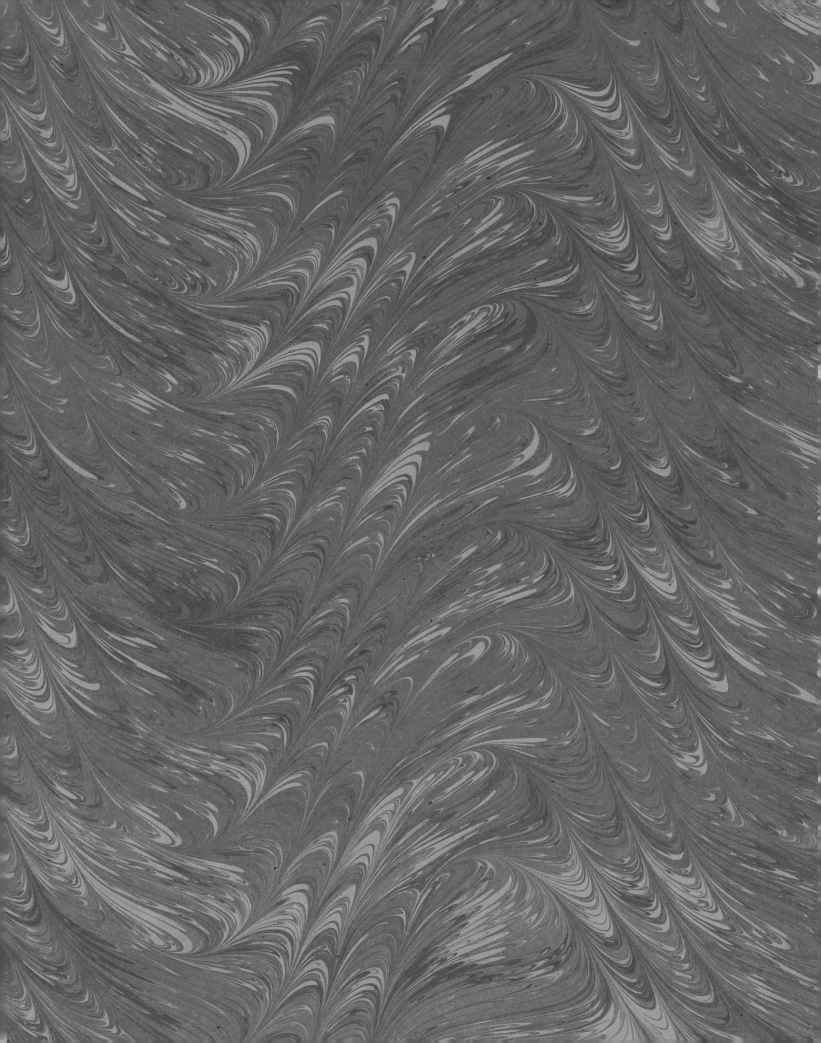